Why?

Leader Guide

WHY?
MAKING SENSE OF GOD'S WILL
LEADER GUIDE

Copyright © 2011 by Abingdon Press
All rights reserved.

This book is printed on elemental chlorine–free paper.
ISBN 978-1-5018-7071-2

18 19 20 21 22 23 24 25 26 27 — 10 9 8 7 6 5 4 3 2 1
MANUFACTURED IN THE UNITED STATES OF AMERICA

ADAM HAMILTON

Why?

Making Sense of God's Will
WITH A NEW INTRODUCTION

LEADER GUIDE
BY SALLY D. SHARPE

ABINGDON PRESS
NASHVILLE

CONTENTS

HOW TO USE THIS
LEADER GUIDE

Why does God allow pain and suffering?
Why do my prayers go unanswered?
Why can't I see God's will for my life?
Why should I trust God when nothing seems to make sense?

We all wrestle with these and similar questions. When we go through tough times—or unexpected joy—it's natural to wonder how (or if) God's will is at work in our world. Even people who are deeply committed to their faith struggle to answer and re-answer these perplexing questions.

Why? Making Sense of God's Will is a book-and-video study intended to help us make sense of these issues by exploring some of the "why" questions we often ask in the face of suffering. It encourages us to be willing to question some of the common assumptions we have about God's will and to consider the ways in which God is at work in our world. The study is not meant to answer all of our questions but to encourage and equip us as we seek to make sense of God's will.

This four-session study may be used by Sunday school classes, as well as by a variety of other small groups meeting at various times during the week. You will want to make group members aware of the accompanying book, which expounds on the video presentations. Participants are strongly encouraged to read the corresponding chapter before the group session. Although the book is not a required part of the study, it will greatly enhance the study experience and serve as a helpful resource to have on hand. Ideally, participants should have the opportunity to purchase copies of the book prior to your first group session.

A QUICK OVERVIEW

As leader, your role will be to facilitate the group sessions using this leader guide and the accompanying DVD. Because no two groups are alike, this guide has been designed to give you flexibility and choice in tailoring the sessions for your group. You may choose one of the following format options, *or adapt these as you wish to meet the schedule and needs of your particular group.* (Note: The times indicated within parentheses are merely estimates. You may move at a faster or slower pace, making adjustments as necessary to fit your schedule.)

Basic Option: 60 minutes
Welcome / Opening Prayer . . . .(3-5 minutes)
Biblical Foundation . . . .(3-5 minutes)
Video Presentation . . . .(15 minutes)
Group Discussion . . . .(30 minutes)
Closing Prayer . . . .(< 5 minutes)

Extended Option: 90 minutes
Welcome / Opening Prayer . . . .(3-5 minutes)
Biblical Foundation . . . .(3-5 minutes)
Opening Activity . . . .(10-15 minutes)
Video Presentation . . . .(15 minutes)
Group Discussion . . . .(30 minutes)
Group Activity . . . .(15 minutes)
Closing Prayer . . . .(< 5 minutes)

You are encouraged to make Scripture and prayer regular components of the group sessions. The Scripture verses provided for each session are intended to serve as a biblical foundation for the group session. Similarly, the opening and closing prayers are intended to "cover" the group session in prayer. Feel free to use the printed prayers or to create your own.

LEADER HELPS

In addition to the session components outlined in the options shown above, this leader guide provides the following "leader helps" to equip you for each group session:

Main Idea	(session theme)
Session Goals	(objectives for the group session)
Key Insights	(summary of main points from the video)
Leader Extra	(additional information related to topic)
Notable Quotation	(noteworthy quote from Adam Hamilton)

You may use these leader helps for your personal preparation only, or you may choose to incorporate them into the group session in some way. For example, you might choose to write the main idea and/or session goals on a board or chart prior to the beginning of the group session, review the key insights from the video either before or after group discussion, incorporate the leader extra into group discussion, or close with the notable quotation.

HELPFUL HINTS

Here are a few helpful hints for preparing and leading the group sessions:

- Become familiar with the material before the group session. If possible, watch the DVD segment in advance.
- Choose the various session components you will use during the group session, including the specific discussion questions you plan to cover. (Highlight these or put a checkmark beside them.) Remember, you do not have to use all of the questions provided, and you even can create your own.
- Secure a TV and DVD player in advance; oversee room setup.

- Begin and end on time.
- Be enthusiastic. Remember, you set the tone for the group.
- Create a climate of participation, encouraging individuals to join in as they feel comfortable.
- Communicate the importance of group discussions and group exercises.
- To stimulate group discussion, consider reviewing the key insights first and then asking participants to tell what they saw as the highlights of the video.
- If no one answers at first, don't be afraid of a little silence. Count to seven silently; then say something such as, "Would anyone like to go first?" If no one responds, venture an answer yourself. Then ask for comments and other responses.
- Model openness as you share with the group. Group members will follow your example. If you share at a surface level, everyone else will follow suit.
- Draw out participants without asking them to share what they are unwilling to share. Make eye contact with someone and say something such as, "How about someone else?"
- Encourage multiple answers or responses before moving on.
- Ask "Why?" or "Why do you believe that?" to help continue a discussion and give it greater depth.
- Affirm others' responses with comments such as, "Great" or "Thanks" or "Good insight"—especially if this is the first time someone has spoken during the group session.
- Give everyone a chance to talk, but keep the conversation moving. Moderate to prevent a few individuals from doing all of the talking.
- Monitor your own contributions. If you are doing most of the talking, back off so that you do not train the group not to respond.
- Remember that you do not need to have all the answers. Your job is to keep the discussion going and to encourage participation.
- Honor the time schedule. If a session is running longer than

10

expected, get consensus from the group before continuing beyond the agreed-upon ending time.

- Consider involving group members in various aspects of the group session, such as asking for volunteers to run the DVD, read the prayers or say their own, read the Scripture, and so forth.

Above all, remember to pray. Pray for God to prepare and guide you; pray for your group members by name and for what God may do in their lives; pray for participants to be sensitive, respectful, and loving in all they say; and pray for God's presence and leading before each group session. Prayer will both encourage and empower you for the weeks ahead.

Now, let's get started!

1. WHY DO THE INNOCENT SUFFER?

*Main Idea: It is possible to reconcile
belief in a loving and powerful God
with the suffering in our world.*

GETTING STARTED

Session Goals
This session is intended to help participants . . .

- carefully reconsider the ideas that everything happens for a reason and that suffering must be the will of God;
- explore the biblical perspective that there is much that happens in our world that is most definitely not the will of God; and
- consider three ideas that provide the foundation for reconciling God's goodness with the suffering in our world.

Welcome / Opening Prayer
Welcome participants and then open the session in prayer. Use the following prayer or offer one of your own:

Lord God, after you created the world, you viewed all that you made and said that everything was "very good." Yet the perfect world you created is not the world in which we now live. Daily we read or hear about disasters, hatred, violence, tragedy, and disease—and often we, or our loved ones, are the ones experiencing these ugly realities. Teach us how we can trust your love when so many bad things happen in our lives and our world. Even when we cannot fully know "why," help us to know the "who" we can depend on—you—remembering that you always are with us and that you promise to give us the strength, grace, and hope we need. Amen.

Biblical Foundation

God created humankind in his image, in the image of God he created them; male and female he created them. God blessed them, and God said to them, "Be fruitful and multiply, and fill the earth and subdue it; and have dominion over the fish of the sea and over the birds of the air and over every living thing that moves upon the earth." (Genesis 1:27-28)

The LORD God took the man and put him in the garden of Eden to till it and keep it. And the LORD God commanded the man, "You may freely eat of every tree of the garden; but of the tree of the knowledge of good and evil you shall not eat, for in the day that you eat of it you shall die." (Genesis 2:15-17)

Opening Activity

Write the following two questions on a board or chart:

- Why does God allow pain and suffering?
- Why did God allow _____?

Acknowledge that human beings have grappled with the first question since the beginning of time and that the question becomes more personal when tragedy, suffering, or difficult times hit close to home. Invite participants to complete the second question by verbally filling in the blank—without going into detail about what happened. Suggest that it might be something that happened to them personally, something that affected one or more persons they love or care about, or something that might have been more distant but still touched them in a personal way for one reason or another. Write their responses on the board or chart.

Key word *theodicy*

4   After everyone has had an opportunity to respond, write the word *theodicy* on the board/chart. Explain that theodicy is the attempt to reconcile belief in a loving and powerful God with the suffering in our world. Say that although you will not be able to resolve the issue in this session, your goal is for the participants to become better equipped to seek answers for themselves.

LEARNING TOGETHER

Video Presentation
Play the DVD segment for Session 1, *Why Do the Innocent Suffer?*
Running Time: 6:50 minutes

Key Insights

1. Theodicy is the attempt to reconcile belief in a loving and powerful God with the suffering in our world.

2. *read* Our disappointment with God in the face of suffering, tragedy, or injustice typically stems from our assumptions about how God is supposed to work in our world. When God does not meet our expectations, we are disappointed, disillusioned, and confused.   *I have seen this happen*

3. The message of the Bible is not a promise that those who believe and do good will not suffer; the Bible is largely a book about people who refused to let go of their faith in the face of suffering.

4. *read* When non-Christians hear Christians say things such as, "Everything happens for a reason" and "It must have been the will of God," they often are left with a picture of a God who wills or causes tragic or evil things to happen.

5. *read* Three foundational ideas can help us reconcile God's goodness with the suffering we experience in our world:

15

read

- God has placed humanity in charge of Earth. God has given human beings the responsibility to "have dominion" over "every living thing that moves upon the earth"—to act on God's behalf in managing, tending, and ruling over the planet. God's primary way of working in the world is through people who are empowered and led by God's Spirit.
- To be human is to be free. God gives human beings the freedom to choose God's way or another way. The ability to choose is an essential part of human existence.
- Human beings have a predisposition to stray from God's path. Our tendency to do what is not God's will is sometimes called the "sin nature."

read discuss

6. Our prescientific ancestors believed that natural disasters are works of God. Today we understand the scientific causes of natural disasters and realize that destructive natural forces are actually essential to life on our planet. This helps us understand why God does not intervene and stop natural disasters from occurring.

7. When God wants to bring hope and help to others, God sends people. Rather than being disappointed with God in the face of tragedy and suffering, we can view the situation as a call to action—to go and be God's hands and voice to those in need.

8. God gives us freedom to make our own decisions, and sometimes those decisions have painful consequences for us and for others. God does not miraculously deliver us from the consequences of our actions or the actions of others.

9. If we have no choices—no free will—we cease to be human and become puppets.

10. Living involves risks, including the risk that we might become sick and die. This is not God's doing; it is simply part of living in a fallen world in which sickness and death are inescapable realities.

11. Rejecting God doesn't change the situation that has caused our suffering; it only removes our greatest source of hope, help, comfort, and strength.

Note: There are numerous books and in-depth studies devoted to the topic of theodicy. Given the expansive nature of the topic, additional Leader Extra material is provided for this session so that you may be better equipped to lead discussion in light of the interests, needs, or questions of your particular group.

Leader Extra
Thoughts About How God Works in the World
Excerpts from *When Christians Get It Wrong,*
by Adam Hamilton

- I believe that God is sovereign—the highest authority, king of the universe—yet God chooses to work in the world in certain ways.
- I believe that God is involved in the affairs of the world but that God does not orchestrate every single circumstance. There is great mystery in this, to be sure.
- The Scriptures testify that God has given us free will; therefore, I do not believe that everything is predetermined by God.
- The Scriptures also affirm that God is just, loving, and kind and tell us that God will not do what is contrary to God's nature. Evil and sin are not from God. Therefore, I do not believe that God ordains or wills everything that happens.
- I believe that although God does not cause pain and suffering and tragedy, God redeems it by working it for our good.[1]

"Much of what we blame God for is the result of humanity's sin and the realities of an imperfect world—such as sickness, disease, natural disasters, accidents, violence, and death. God accepts these realities, but God does not initiate them. . . .

17

"When it comes to the problem of suffering, we must allow room for mystery, knowing that there is much we do not know and cannot understand."[2]

Leader Extra
God's Sovereignty and Determinism
Excerpt from *When Christians Get It Wrong,* by Adam Hamilton

This term [sovereignty] means that God is the highest authority, there is no one to whom God reports and no one to whom God answers. God is the Supreme Ruler—the "King of the Universe." The universe is the rightful property of God, who created it. Nearly all Christians would agree that God is sovereign—the highest authority and not dependent upon anything or anyone else.

In an attempt to glorify God, however, some people go too far. They claim that God is not only the highest authority but also the 'Supreme Micromanager.' They would never use this phrase to describe God, but this is what their picture of God looks like. They suggest that God is actually controlling every dimension of creation. This is sometimes referred to as 'determinism.' The logical outcome of this line of reasoning...makes God a monster.

...I believe all creation is sustained by God and draws its existence from God. But if God does exercise this kind of [micromanager] control, it raises a host of questions.... Why would God create human beings with the appearance of freedom and a longing for freedom if God is going to control every thought, every word, and every action behind the scenes? And if God controls everything we do, which also implies that God determines the outcome of all things, what is the point of exerting any effort? . . .

This leads to another assumption—that history unfolds according to God's predetermined plan.... We have the illusion of making our own choices, but in fact we do no such thing because God has predetermined exactly what will happen, and we cannot change it....

Most people become deeply troubled by this picture of God controlling everything when they encounter horrific evil…. I believe God is able to redeem suffering and bring good from evil; but to say that God planned, willed, and prompted the hearts of those who committed…a heinous crime in order to accomplish some greater good strikes me as the worst kind of blasphemy. No ends could justify such terrible means. To claim such an act is the will of God is to say that God is neither loving nor just.[3]

Leader Extra
The Mystery of God's Sovereignty and Our Free Will

read

It is impossible for us to understand fully the dynamics of God's sovereignty and our free will. Scripture is clear that God knows all things (Psalm 139:1-4; Matthew 6:8; 24:36) and is sovereign (Colossians 1:16-17; Daniel 4:35). The Bible also says that we have the freedom to choose and are held responsible for our actions (Genesis 2:15-17; Romans 3:19). How these facts work together is impossible for our finite minds to comprehend (Romans 11:33-36).

People sometimes take one of two extremes in regard to this question. Some emphasize the sovereignty of God to the point that human beings are little more than puppets doing what they have been programmed to do. Others emphasize free will to the point of God not being sovereign above all. Yet neither of these positions is congruent with the nature and character of God revealed through the Scriptures. The Scriptures reveal a God who is both Sovereign Ruler, reigning over all, and Loving Parent, giving us the ability to exercise free will and make choices. How these two dynamics work together remains a mystery. And without mystery, there can be no real faith.

Leader Extra
Suffering and God's Discipline

Some Christians say that suffering is part of God's plan because God needs to discipline or teach us. A Scripture passage often cited in support of this view is Hebrews 12:4-11:

> In your struggle against sin you have not yet resisted to the point of shedding your blood. And you have forgotten the exhortation that addresses you as children— "My child, do not regard lightly the discipline of the Lord, or lose heart when you are punished by him; for the Lord disciplines those whom he loves, and chastises every child whom he accepts." Endure trials for the sake of discipline. God is treating you as children; for what child is there whom a parent does not discipline? If you do not have that discipline in which all children share, then you are illegitimate and not his children. Moreover, we had human parents to discipline us, and we respected them. Should we not be even more willing to be subject to the Father of spirits and live? For they disciplined us for a short time as seemed best to them, but he disciplines us for our good, in order that we may share his holiness. Now, discipline always seems painful rather than pleasant at the time, but later it yields the peaceful fruit of righteousness to those who have been trained by it. (Hebrews 12:4-11)

Other Christians say that God does not cause difficult and tragic experiences in order to teach us a lesson; rather, God uses them to refine us, improve us, and make us more like Christ. (Some say God allows suffering for this redemptive purpose.) They suggest that, like a loving parent, God turns the difficult and painful experiences of our lives into opportunities for teaching, strengthening, encouraging, and loving us. Romans 8:28-29 supports the view that God uses all circumstances, including difficult ones, to conform us into the image of Christ:

> And we know that in all things God works for the good of those who love him, who have been called according to his purpose. For

20

those God foreknew he also predestined to be conformed to the likeness of his Son, that he might be the firstborn among many brothers. (Romans 8:28-29 NIV)

Leader Extra
New Testament Insights on Suffering
Excerpt from When Christians Get It Wrong, Leader Guide, by Adam Hamilton

Matthew 14:13-21
This story is typical of many. When Jesus met people with problems (whether illness, hunger, or any of the many other challenges humans face), he did not offer them a lecture about what they'd done wrong, or tell them God was teaching them a lesson. Instead, he had compassion and sought to make things better.

Luke 13:1-17
In Jesus' day, as in ours, many people were inclined to view tragedy and suffering as a divine punishment and/or object lesson. Jesus said they "got it wrong." He recognized the randomness of some tragedies and the role of evil in creating others. He was not interested in assigning blame but in bringing healing.

John 9:1-41
Jesus' disciples began this story convinced that the man they saw begging was born blind due either to his own or his parents' sins. When the story ended, the Pharisees were still sure of that (verse 34). Again, Jesus disagreed. God, he said, can bring good even out of tragedy, but that does not mean God caused it.

Romans 8:18-28, 35-39
Christians have sometimes applied this passage, especially verse 28, in hurtful ways. Note that verse 28 does NOT say God causes all things, nor that everything that happens is good. Instead, Paul affirms his triumphant faith that if we put our lives in God's hands, God will work for good IN all things.

<u>2 Corinthians 4:5-18</u>
The apostle Paul's language soars as he expresses his unshakable trust in the goodness of God's purposes. What matters most, he says, is not what's happening outside us. We look to the unseen, and we know that God is always at work, renewing us inwardly no matter what circumstances we face.

<u>1 Peter 5:6-10</u>
Early Christian believers often faced persecution from the Roman government, alienation from their families, and economic hardship. Peter was convinced that God did not cause these hardships, and that God was still present and working for good even when believers suffered.[4]

For Further Study
Leslie Weatherhead's *The Will of God* (Abingdon, 1999) is a classic on the subject of God's will and would prove to be a helpful resource. Rebecca Laird's *The Will of God: A Workbook* (Abingdon, 1995) is an excellent small-group study based on Weatherhead's book.

Group Discussion
Note: More questions are provided than you may have time for. Select those you would like your group to discuss.

1. How do our assumptions about how God is supposed to work in the world affect the way we feel when we are faced with injustice, tragedy, or suffering? Why is it important to question our assumptions about how God works in the world?
2. Have you (or someone you know) ever thought that if you were a good person, God would take care of you and nothing bad would happen? How did your (or their) thoughts and feelings change when something bad happened? What are your beliefs about how God works in the world? (See "Leader Extra: Thoughts About How God Works in the World.")
3. Read John 16:33. What did Jesus ask of God on behalf of his followers? In contrast to those who feel that "being good" is

a kind of "suffering insurance," what did Jesus say? What is your reaction to his words? How can you "take heart" because Jesus has overcome the world—in other words, what would this look like in your day-to-day life?

4. Name and discuss several characters from the Bible who refused to let go of their faith in the face of suffering. How did these individuals demonstrate their faith despite their circumstances? What do you think fueled their faith?

5. Do you believe that everything happens for a reason? Why or why not? How might this statement be more upsetting than comforting to someone who is in the midst of pain or suffering? What do you believe such a statement implies about God or God's will?

6. On pages 6-7 of *Why? Making Sense of God's Will*, Adam Hamilton writes, "When a young woman is raped and murdered, was this really the will of God? Did God write this into the woman's life story . . . ? If God wished for this to happen, then God must have put it into the heart of the murderer to do this terrible thing. Does that sound like a just or loving God? The person who committed this crime will be put in prison as a murdering monster, but by saying 'It must have been the will of God,' we affirm that God intended this event to happen." Share your thoughts in response to this example.

7. What does it mean to say that God is sovereign? (See "Leader Extra: God's Sovereignty and Determinism.")

8. Some say that if God is sovereign—having ultimate authority and control—then God must not be a loving God. Others argue that if God is all-loving, then God must not have all power and authority. Still others find a middle ground, affirming God's ultimate authority and rule while acknowledging God's loving choice to give us free will. Do you believe it is possible for God to be both all-powerful and all-loving? Explain your response. (See "Leader Extra: The Mystery of God's Sovereignty and Our Free Will.")

9. What is the difference between punishment and discipline? How would you explain or describe the discipline of a loving

Charlie's sermon   23

parent? Read aloud from: "Leader Extra: Suffering and God's Discipline." What is the difference between the two viewpoints described? Do you believe it is ever appropriate to view suffering as God's discipline? Why or why not?

10. Read Genesis 1:27-28. According to this passage, what responsibility has God given to us? Thankfully, God did not leave us to our own devices to carry out this responsibility. What did God set in motion to help give order and predictability to creation? What did God give to human beings to equip us for our charge? (See pages 10-12 in *Why? Making Sense of God's Will.*)

11. What is God's primary way of acting in the world? What are some biblical and contemporary or current examples?

12. Read Genesis 2:15. What does the tree in the garden represent? Why is free will—the ability to choose—so important to us as human beings? How is the gift of free will an expression of God's love?

13. The Hebrew and Greek words most frequently translated as the English word sin mean to stray from the path. How would you describe this tendency within us to stray from the path? What evidence do you find in yourself, and in the world around you, that human beings have a predisposition to reject God's will?

14. What has God done, according to the Scriptures, to lead humanity away from the wrong and to do what is right?

15. How did prescientific people explain natural disasters? What do we know today about earthquakes, monsoons, and other destructive forces of nature that helps us understand why God does not intervene and stop these things from occurring?

16. The author writes, "Natural disasters and widespread poverty that affect so many in our world are a call to action" (*Why?*, page 19). When was a time you viewed a natural disaster or tragedy as a call to action? How did you respond?

17. When has a decision that you made resulted in painful consequences—for you and/or others? When has the decision of someone else brought pain or suffering into your life?

18. What would a world look like where God directly controls all things—where human freedom is restricted so that we never do the wrong thing and tragedies never happen? Would you want to live in such a world? Why or why not?

19. Why do you think many people view human sickness as a punishment from God? Respond to the following statement: "I suggest that if we take seriously the idea that Jesus Christ bore on the cross the punishment for sin, then we should be very careful when suggesting that God has made us sick" (*Why?*, page 25).

20. When we become ill, we can blame God or draw comfort from the fact that God walks with us through the journey. Most of us know people who have chosen each response. How would you compare the experience of someone who blamed God for his or her illness to that of someone who took comfort in walking with God and placing his or her life in God's hands?

21. When have you been angry with God? How can shouting at God be an act of faith? Why is expressing anger or hurt to God an important part of the grieving or healing process?

22. What do you think is lost when someone rejects God in the face of suffering?

Group Activity

Option 1: Return the group's focus to the responses you wrote on the board or chart during the Opening Activity. Say: *You are not alone in asking why. Suffering has always raised deep spiritual questions. The Book of Job teaches that we can't always explain suffering. Job struggled with great pain and loss, and he discovered that he needed more than the "why" answers he asked God for—which never came. In the end, Job found lasting trust in a God bigger and wiser than he was.*

Divide into two groups and assign each group the following Scriptures and related questions. Once the groups have had time to discuss, come back together and have each group share their responses.

<u>Group 1</u>
Scripture: Job 1:21; 2:1-7
Questions: Who do you think causes suffering? Some think Job 1:21 means that God caused Job's agony. Do you think that fits the rest of the story? Why or why not? How can this verse be seen as an expression of Job's trust in God's eternal love? To what extent do you share that trust?

<u>Group 2</u>
Scripture: Job 42:7
Questions: According to God, did Job's friends speak "rightly"? Have well-meaning friends ever given glib explanations of your suffering? How did their explanations make you feel? How can God's presence with you help more than any explanation?

Option 2: In advance of the session, read "Leader Extra: New Testament Insights on Suffering." Choose several of the passages to explore as a whole group. Ask a participant to read one of the passages aloud; then read aloud or paraphrase the corresponding commentary from the Leader Extra. Invite participants to share any additional insights they have. Then move on to the next Scripture passage, continuing in the same manner.

WRAPPING UP

Notable Quotation
When God wants to bring hope and help to others, God sends people. Much of the suffering in our world is because God's people have yet to hear or answer God's call to go and to be God's hands and voice. . . .
—Adam Hamilton

26

Closing Prayer

Dear God, there is so much pain and suffering and heartache in this world. We know we live in a fallen, imperfect world, and yet we struggle to make sense of it all. When pain and suffering touch our lives, we find ourselves asking why. Sometimes we grasp for answers or explanations that only wind up causing more pain and confusion. Other times we get angry and question your love for us. Help us to sort through our questions, reexamine our assumptions, and cling to the unshakable truths that you love us and are with us always. Teach us not to interpret your love according to our circumstances, but to interpret our circumstances according to your love, remembering that you promise to bring good from it all. Amen.

2. WHY DO MY PRAYERS GO UNANSWERED?

*Main Idea: Prayer is not primarily about intercession.
It is about a relationship with God.*

GETTING STARTED

Session Goals
This session is intended to help participants . . .

- grapple with the question of why God sometimes is silent when we cry out to God in our time of greatest need;
- see that our typical way of understanding prayer—telling God what we want God to do and then expecting God to do what we ask—is illogical and bound to leave us disappointed;
- recognize that unanswered prayer is not the result of what we do wrong when we pray;
- gain new insight into Jesus' teachings about prayer;
- explore two New Testament prayers that went unanswered and what they teach us about prayer;
- consider the purpose of prayer, how God answers prayer, and what we should pray for; and
- understand that prayer is about a relationship, not a transaction.

Opening Prayer
Lord God, we live in a me-centered, fast-paced world. We tend to want results, and we want them on our timetable. We get frustrated and

29

discouraged when our prayers are not answered—at least not in the way that we want. Remind us today that you are not a vending machine and that prayer is not a transaction. Help us to understand that prayer is about our relationship with you; it is the way we relate to you and grow closer to you. Teach us to value a different kind of result from prayer—an inner result that takes place in our spirits when we talk with you regularly. Amen.

Biblical Foundation

O my God, I cry by day, but you do not answer;
and by night, but find no rest. (Psalm 22:2)

If you remain in me and my words remain in you, ask for whatever you want and it will be done for you. (John 15:7 CEB)

Father, if you are willing, remove this cup from me; yet, not my will but yours be done. (Luke 22:42)

Truly I tell you, if you have faith and do not doubt, . . . even if you say to this mountain, "Be lifted up and thrown into the sea," it will be done. Whatever you ask for in prayer with faith, you will receive. (Matthew 21:21-22)

Opening Activity
Option 1: Write the following statements on a board or chart:

> I prayed and prayed, but my prayer wasn't answered.
> If my prayers don't change anything, why bother?

Read each statement aloud, one at a time, and ask participants to raise their hands if they have ever felt that way. Then ask participants if they can recall any unanswered prayers that now, years later, they are thankful God did not answer as they had requested. You might begin the sharing by giving an example from your own life or reading the example given by the author about a man in his congregation (Why?, page 45). Invite participants to share as they are willing. Then say: Today we will consider how prayer works and explore why our typical understanding of prayer—telling God what we want God to do and then expecting God to do what we ask—is illogical and bound to leave us disappointed.

Option 2: In advance, write each of the prayer quotations from "Leader Extra: Famous Quotations on Prayer" on a separate sheet of paper or poster board, and place them all over the front wall of the room. Ask each participant to pick one quotation and share why that quotation speaks to her or him about prayer.

LEARNING TOGETHER

Video Presentation
Play the DVD segment for Session 2, *Why Do My Prayers Go Unanswered?*
Running Time: 6:45 minutes

Key Insights
1. Many people struggle with their faith because of God's silence when they cry out to God in their time of greatest need.
2. Our expectations about prayer are shaped in part by Jesus' words in a handful of passages, including Matthew 21:21-22. Jesus' words in these verses seem to promise that God will do whatever we ask provided we have faith; however, they take on different meaning when we view them as a hyperbolic statement meant to be taken seriously but not literally. Jesus was inviting his followers to pray boldly and with faith, trusting God for the outcome—as opposed to encouraging them to ask whatever they might want and expecting God to grant their request.
3. Unanswered prayer is not the result of what we do wrong when we pray; it is not the result of our failure to live for Christ, to confess our sin, or to have enough faith.
4. When the apostle Paul prayed for God to remove a thorn in his flesh, God's response was not healing but an assurance of

31

the sufficiency of God's grace. Paul came to see that every difficulty was an opportunity for God to work in perfecting his soul and in accomplishing good through him.

5. Jesus asked God to deliver him from suffering, but God did not. As Jesus hung on the cross, no doubt he felt the absence of God and the disappointment we sometimes feel when our prayers go unanswered. Yet we know that God did not forsake Jesus; God used Jesus' suffering and death for the redemption of the world.

6. God does not always answer our prayers (in the way that we want), even when we offer them in faith. Yet God never abandons us. God works through every situation, redeeming it and bringing good from it (Romans 8:28, NIV).

7. Miracles are miracles because they are rare. God sometimes miraculously and directly intervenes in the world, but God's customary way of working in our lives is through the ordinary. Rather than suspending the laws of nature that God created and bypassing the human beings God created to do God's work, God typically works through natural laws and through people.

8. God intends us to be the answers to one another's prayers. Our task is to pay attention, listen for the promptings of the Spirit, and then act to help and bless others.

9. God will not suspend or violate another person's free will in order to answer our prayers.

10. In the face of suffering or adversity, God's answer to our prayers is often not to deliver us or others from the suffering, but to walk with us through it and then to transform it to bring good.

11. We need to be very careful in how we express thanks following deliverance from tragedy; however, whether God directly intervenes in a given situation or indirectly works through creative power, we know that all good and perfect gifts come from God.

12. Prayer is not primarily about intercession; it is about entering into a relationship with God and yielding our lives to God.

Leader Extra
Jesus' Practice of Prayer

Philip Yancey has written that "the simplest answer to the question 'Why pray?' is 'Because Jesus did'" (*Prayer: Does It Make Any Difference?*; Zondervan, 2010; page 78). Many of our questions about prayer (for example, "Doesn't God already know what I need?") don't seem to have troubled Jesus. He simply knew that keeping a strong connection with God called for a lot of prayer. We can learn much about the practice of prayer from Jesus' example:

But he would withdraw to deserted places and pray. (Luke 5:16)

In the morning, while it was still very dark, he got up and went out to a deserted place, and there he prayed. (Mark 1:35)

And after he had dismissed the crowds, he went up the mountain by himself to pray. When evening came, he was there alone. (Matthew 14:23)

In these verses, we see that Jesus . . .

- prayed regularly,
- spent time with God alone,
- sought quiet, solitary places where he would not be disturbed,
- prayed in the morning to begin his day, and
- prayed in the evening, after a hard day's work.

Leader Extra
Persistence in Prayer

Often Jesus' parables taught by similarity: "God is like this familiar activity or thing." In the parable of the unjust judge, found in Luke 18:1-8, Jesus taught by contrast: "God is not like this unjust judge. If even a bad judge can be persuaded, imagine how much more God wants to listen to your prayers." The real question, said Jesus, is not about God, but us: "Will the Son of Man find faith on the earth?" Jesus wanted his followers to learn that they should always pray and not give up.

Persistence in prayer can be challenging when God appears to be slow in answering. Yet 2 Peter 3:8-9 tells us that "the Lord is not slow in keeping his promise" (NIV), for a thousand years are as one day to God. Likewise, in the parable of the unjust judge, Jesus links the idea of God "quickly" giving us justice to his promised future return. Clearly God has a different understanding of time than we do. Sometimes we find it difficult to maintain our faith and trust, given what we perceive as the pace of God's patient love for us. Yet we can find encouragement in remembering that God sees the "big picture" from the perspective of eternity, and that God's patient love is something we would not want to be without.

Leader Extra
Famous Quotations on Prayer

"To be a Christian without prayer is no more possible than to be alive without breathing."—Martin Luther King, Jr.

"In prayer it is better to have a heart without words than words without a heart."—Mahatma Gandhi

"Pray as though everything depended on God. Work as though everything depended on you." —Saint Augustine

"Courage is fear that has said its prayers."—Dorothy Bernard

"Pray, and let God worry."—Martin Luther

"Prayer is as natural an expression of faith as breathing is of life." —Jonathan Edwards

"All prayers are answered if we are willing to admit that sometimes the answer is 'no.'"—unknown

"Grant that I may not pray alone with the mouth; help me that I may pray from the depths of my heart."—Martin Luther

"Many people pray as if God were a big aspirin pill; they come only when they hurt."—B. Graham Dienert

"I have had prayers answered—most strangely so sometimes—but I think our heavenly Father's loving-kindness has been even more evident in what He has refused me."—Lewis Carroll

"Pray often; for prayer is a shield to the soul, a sacrifice to God, and a scourge for Satan."—John Bunyan

"Prayer is where the action is."—John Wesley

"I have been driven many times upon my knees by the overwhelming conviction that I had nowhere else to go."—Abraham Lincoln

"God speaks in the silence of the heart. Listening is the beginning of prayer."—Mother Teresa

Group Discussion
Note: More questions are provided than you will have time for. Select those you would like your group to discuss.

1. Some Christians claim that God regularly answers their prayers for things that seem of no consequence. Do you believe that God answers prayers for things such as parking spaces and touchdown passes? If so, what would you say to someone whose fervent prayers for a loved one with cancer have not been answered? Explain your response.
2. Read Matthew 21:21-22. What does Jesus seem to promise in these verses? In what way is this problematic? What are some common reasons people offer in an attempt to explain why prayers might go unanswered? What did Jesus' own acts of healing reveal about any "requirements" necessary for

God to act on our behalf? (See Mark 10:46-51 and Luke 7:11-17.)

3. What is faith, and why is it important in prayer? Do you believe we must have enough faith in order for our prayers to be answered? Why or why not? Read Mark 9:14-29 and Matthew 17:14-21. What do these verses tell us about how much faith is necessary for answered prayer?

4. What is hyperbole? How did Jesus use hyperbole when he spoke and taught, and for what purpose? Discuss the following examples: Matthew 5:29-30; 19:24; Mark 10:25; Luke 18:25. Now reread Matthew 21:22. How might these words be seen as a hyperbolic statement? What is the challenge of applying Jesus' words in these verses literally?

5. Read 2 Corinthians 12:7-10. What did Paul ask of God three times, and what was God's response? How did the experience strengthen Paul's faith, rather than weaken it? Have you ever experienced a weakness that made you stronger? What does "my grace is sufficient for you" mean in everyday terms?

6. Read Luke 22:39-42. What did Jesus ask of God? How do we know that Jesus was willing to accept God's choice not to intervene? Does fear of disappointment ever keep you from asking God for what you wish and hope for? How can you follow Jesus' example in praying about a concern (big or small) that is on your heart right now?

7. Read Matthew 6:8. What common reason or excuse for not praying is expressed in this verse? Have you ever felt that prayer was unnecessary or pointless? Explain your response. If God already knows our needs before we ask, why should we pray?

8. Read aloud "Leader Extra: Jesus' Practice of Prayer." What strikes you about the timing, settings, frequency, or intensity of Jesus' prayers? When, where, and how often do you pray? What are one or two changes you could make in your pattern or practice of prayer in order to bring you closer to Jesus' pattern?

9. Read Philippians 4:4-7. What does the apostle Paul say results from presenting our requests to God in prayer? How does

knowing that Paul was in prison and facing possible execution when he wrote these words inform your understanding of Paul's words?

10. In Philippians 4:7, Paul says that God's peace "surpasses all understanding." In what ways does our wish to figure things out through our own reasoning sometimes rob us of peace? Have you ever prayed about something and then experienced the peace that Paul describes? Share as you are willing.

11. Read Luke 18:1-8, followed by "Leader Extra: Persistence in Prayer." Have you ever persisted in prayer about a particular concern? If so, what effect(s) did the experience have on you? What are the things that make you most likely to give up praying? What experiences or beliefs lead you to persist in prayer?

12. Do you believe God still works miracles today? Have you or someone you know ever witnessed a miraculous intervention of God?

13. According to the author, what is the way that God typically works in the world? What does it mean to say that God intends us to be the answers to one another's prayers? How is this possible?

14. Why do you think God sometimes does not deliver us from suffering but, instead, walks with us through it? How can unanswered prayer lead to events that change us, others, and/or the world? Share a personal example or story, if you can. How have you experienced the truth of Romans 8:28 in your own life?

15. If we shouldn't blame God for the bad things that happen, why should we give God credit for the good things that happen? Read James 1:17. What insight does this verse give us?

16. In what ways do we demonstrate that we tend to view prayer more as a transaction than a relationship? How would you explain the purpose of prayer?

17. What can we do to make sure we pray more often? Are there places or things that help or remind you to pray (for example, candles, a special place in your home, a cross, other)?

18. (Note: Skip this item if you plan to do option 2 of the opening activity.) In advance, write each of the prayer quotations from "Leader Extra: Famous Quotations on Prayer" on a separate sheet of paper or poster board, and place them all over the front wall of the room. Ask each participant to pick one quotation and share why that quotation speaks to her or him about prayer.

Group Activity

Have someone read aloud Luke 12:4. Ask: *What did Jesus tell us not to fear?* Then have someone read aloud Hebrews 2:15. Ask: *According to this verse, what did Jesus come to do?*

Point out that our fear—particularly our fear of death—causes us to be concerned about this life and the things of the world. Have participants name everyday issues they are concerned about (money, work, school, houses, cars, illness/health issues). Draw a line down the middle of a board or chart and write their concerns on the left side as they name them. As you do the activity and discussion below, write the group's responses on the right side of the board or chart.

Have someone read aloud Ephesians 6:10-20. Say: *This passage points us to what is really important—not this life and the things of the world, but the unseen spiritual world in which God reigns. The apostle Paul calls us to see beyond the haze of everyday life to God's kingdom beyond. He calls us to put on our spiritual armor and stand firmly against the forces of evil and the world. Prayer is what connects us to the spiritual world. Through prayer we tap into God's power, which is always available to help us.*

Discuss: *What can spiritual armor do for us? Although we cannot completely shut ourselves off from the cares of this world—or totally eliminate all our fears—how can we raise our gaze beyond the worries of the world and focus more of our energy on the reality of God's world? How can prayer help us to do this?*

Challenge each participant to identify one prayer step he or she can take this week to connect more fully with God.

WRAPPING UP

Notable Quotation

I have . . . learned over the years that, in the face of suffering or adversity, God's answer to my prayers is often not to deliver me or others from the suffering, but to walk with me or them through it, and then to transform it and use it to change my life, their lives, or the world.

—Adam Hamilton

Closing Prayer

Loving and compassionate God, we praise you for being our Father, our Protector, and our Provider. Although we do not understand why some prayers are answered and others are not, we know from Scripture and from the living testimony of Jesus that you are compassionate, loving, just, and good. We also know that you have promised to be with us always and to work in all things for our good. Help us to trust you and to yield our wills and our very lives to you, just as Jesus did. Teach us to spend more time in prayer focusing on our relationship with you and your Kingdom priorities. Remind us to pray often, and show us the power of prayer to shape our lives. Amen.

3. WHY CAN'T I SEE GOD'S WILL FOR MY LIFE?

*Main Idea: Our lives are less like a script and more
like a blank book where the remaining chapters
are yet to be written; God's desire is to lead us
and to collaborate with us in pursuing
God's plan for our lives.*

GETTING STARTED

Session Goals
This session is intended to help participants . . .

- consider two important questions related to God's will:
  - ≈ Is God's will a set of principles and precepts we live by, or does God have a specific will for each decision we make, every action we take, and every word we speak?
  - ≈ Is everything that happens predetermined by God and bound to take place, or does God give us freedom to resist God's will and plans?
- explore how we can know God's will for our lives;
- consider that we are invited to collaborate with God in writing the story of our lives;
- recognize that in any given situation, God wills that we do the most loving thing and that the principles and precepts by which we know the loving thing are found in the Scriptures; and
- see that God regularly guides us if we listen and pay attention.

41

Opening Prayer

Almighty God, we want to live our lives in a way that pleases you, that conforms to your will. But discerning your will is not always easy! Teach us how we can know your will. Direct our minds, hearts, hands, and feet so that we might truly be your disciples. Live in and through us so that we might collaborate with you as we live out our lives, accomplishing your work in the world as we love and serve others. In Jesus' name we pray. Amen.

Biblical Foundation

We haven't stopped praying for you and asking for you to be filled with the knowledge of God's will, . . . so that you can live lives that are worthy of the Lord and pleasing to him in every way: by producing fruit in every good work and growing in the knowledge of God. (Colossians 1:9-10, CEB)

So, brothers and sisters, because of God's mercies, I encourage you to present your bodies as a living sacrifice that is holy and pleasing to God. This is your appropriate priestly service. Don't be conformed to the patterns of this world, but be transformed by the renewing of your minds so that you can figure out what God's will is—what is good and pleasing and mature. (Romans 12:1-2, CEB)

Opening Activity

Option 1: Read Colossians 1:9-10. Ask: *According to the apostle Paul, what is the purpose of knowing God's will? How would you explain to someone why it is important to seek and to know the will of God?*

Option 2: In advance, write each of the quotations from "Leader Extra: Famous Quotations on God's Will" on a separate sheet of paper or poster board, and place them all over the front wall of the room. Ask each participant to pick one quotation and share why that quotation speaks to her or him about God's will—or have them break into pairs for sharing if your group is large.

LEARNING TOGETHER

Video Presentation

Play the DVD segment for Session 3, *Why Can't I See God's Will for My Life?*
Running Time: 7:03 minutes

Key Insights

1. Some believe that God's plan is written in advance, like a manuscript for a play. There are several logical problems with this view:
   - If everything happens according to God's predetermined plan, then God is ultimately responsible for all the evil and injustice throughout human history.
   - If we are merely acting in a play God has already written, there is no point in life. We have the illusion of freedom but are really pawns moved by the hand of God.
   - If we are merely following the script God wrote, there is no justice in God's punishing us for something God has prede termined or forced us to do.
2. A second view is that God has a perfect plan for our lives. This introduces another problem: God's perfect will is seldom so clear that we can't miss it, which means we are left to try to discover it. Though this view distinguishes between God's "perfect will" and God's "permissive will"—which allows for things that are not what God ideally plans for us but are acceptable to God—one would need to stray from God's perfect plan only once to throw off the rest of the plan.
3. A third view is that God has an idea and outline for the story of our lives and invites us to collaborate in filling in the outline with God each day. Every decision, every encounter, every challenge is an opportunity for us to collaborate with God in writing our story. And when we invite God to collaborate with us, our story becomes one of redemption and love and hope.
4. God is like a Heavenly Parent who, rather than predetermining

43

our actions, provides advice and wisdom, hoping that in everything we will seek to love God and neighbor.

5. God's will is more about how we make our decisions than about the specific decisions we make. This sense of God's will is called God's prescriptive will; it is the instruction God has given us in the Bible that will lead to greater spiritual and relational health.

6. According to the apostle Paul, the purpose of knowing God's will is that we might "live a life worthy of the Lord" and grow in the "knowledge of God" (Colossians 1:9-10 CEB).

7. We have opportunities each day to be used as instruments of God's love and grace. Collaborating with God is inviting God to lead us, guide us, and use us; it requires paying attention and saying yes to those moments when our story can be part of God's larger redemption story.

8. God has given us tools to help us discern God's will: Scripture and the work of the Holy Spirit, other Christians, our pastors and leaders, and our own intellect and common sense.

9. The will of God is not our happiness but our faithfulness. God's plan may not be the easiest path and may actually lead to hardship, difficulty, and suffering. But there is joy in hardship when we know we are in the middle of God's will.

Leader Extra
Famous Quotations on God's Will

"We're not necessarily doubting that God will do the best for us; we are wondering how painful the best will turn out to be"—C. S. Lewis

"True holiness consists in doing God's will with a smile."—Mother Teresa

"God will not suffer man to have a knowledge of things to come; for if he had prescience of his prosperity, he would be careless; and if understanding of his adversity, he would be despairing and senseless."
—Saint Augustine

"We can only learn to know ourselves and do what we can—namely, surrender our will and fulfill God's will in us."—St. Teresa of Avila

"When God and his glory are made our end, we shall find a silent likeness pass in upon us; the beauty of God will, by degrees, enter upon our soul."—Stephen Charnock

"I just want to do God's will. And He's allowed me to go up to the mountain. And I've looked over. And I've seen the Promised Land." —Martin Luther King, Jr.

"Someone once described the contrast between a good life and a godly life as the difference between the top of the ocean and the bottom. On top, sometimes it's like glass—serene and calm—and other times it's raging and stormy. But hundreds of fathoms below, it is beautiful and consistent, always calm, always peaceful."—Bill McCartney

Leader Extra
Sanctification

The Holman Bible Dictionary says that sanctification is "the process of being made holy, resulting in a changed life-style for the believer. The English word *sanctification* comes from the Latin *santificatio*, meaning the act/process of making holy, consecrated." Many Christians speak of sanctification as the process of being conformed into the image of Jesus Christ.

John Wesley, founder of Methodism, defined *sanctification* as "going on to perfection" and growing in love of God and neighbor. He believed that this process begins after justification by faith and that it happens gradually for most people. His book *A Plain Account of Christian Perfection* is a defense of his position on the doctrine of Christian perfection or sanctification (see http://gbgm-umc.org/UMhistory/Wesley/perfect.html).

Leader Extra
Tools to Help Us Discern God's Will

When we are making decisions or seeking to know God's will, we can use four tools that God has given us:

1) The gift of Scripture and the work of the Holy Spirit
2) Pastors and leaders in the church—both present and past—who serve as guides
3) Our own intellect and common sense
4) Other Christians and life experiences through whom God may speak to us

The Wesleyan quadrilateral speaks of these four tools using the language of Scripture, tradition, reason, and experience. God uses each of these tools to speak to us and give us guidance, instruction, and direction.

It is important not to rely on one of these tools to the exclusion of the others, but to use them all as checks and balances. An important guideline is that God will never lead or direct us in a way that contradicts God's Word. In particular, the life and teachings of Jesus, who is the clearest expression we have of God, provide invaluable insight and instruction for us as we seek to discern God's will and live godly lives.

Key point

Leader Extra
Spiritual Gifts and Finding God's Will for Your Life

The discovery and acknowledgment of our individual gifts and talents can be a great comfort and help in our quest to discover God's will for our lives. Knowing how God has gifted and "shaped" each of us can help us find our special place in Christ's family.

Suggest to participants that a good beginning point is to read about the gifts in Romans 12, 1 Corinthians 12, and Ephesians 4. Next, they should ask themselves questions such as:

What can I do that many other people cannot?

<u>What am I passionate about?</u>
<u>What energizes me and gives me great joy?</u>

It is helpful to list all of the talents, skills, and gifts they come up with. Then they may tell several Christian friends what they are doing and ask them to review the list and suggest anything that might have been overlooked. The final step is to prayerfully consider how these gifts can be applied to their life in Christ.

There are numerous studies on spiritual gifts and spiritual gifts inventories that can assist us in discerning our gifts. *Serving from the Heart* is an excellent resource for individuals and groups. A gifts discovery tool is included in the resource and also may be found at http://ministrymatters.agroupmail.com/spiritual gifts.

Group Discussion

Note: More questions are provided than you may have time for. Select those you would like your group to discuss.

1. Compare and contrast the following three views of God's will, noting any challenges or questions raised by each. (You might want to make three columns on a board or chart and write responses as participants share them. Label the columns "Written in Advance," "Perfect Plan With Choices Allowed," and "Collaboration.")

   • God's plan is written in advance, like a manuscript for a play.

   • God has a perfect plan for our lives, yet God allows us to make choices that are not what God ideally plans for us but are acceptable.

   • God has an idea and outline for the story of our lives and invites us to collaborate in filling in the outline with God each day.

   Which view more closely represents your own view, and why?

2. Read Proverbs 3:1-6. What does it mean to trust in the Lord with all your heart and not to rely on your own understanding? Does this mean that God will make your decisions for

47

you? What can you expect from God when facing decisions? In what way is trust the beginning of knowing God's will for your life?

3. How does the analogy of a loving parent help us understand God's will for our lives? As our Heavenly Parent, how does God help us find our way in life? What are God's expectations or hopes for us?

4. Do you believe God's will is more about how we make our decisions than about the specific decisions we make? Why or why not?

5. What is God's prescriptive will? How has God's prescriptive will helped you when making an important decision in your life?

6. What does it mean to "collaborate" with God? How does collaborating with God affect not only our own lives but also the lives of others? What opportunities have you had to be an instrument of God's love and grace in others' lives? How has God used others in this role in your own life?

7. What tools has God given us to help us discern God's will? (See "Leader Extra: Tools to Help Us Discern God's Will.") Are there other tools that might also help? Why is it important to use all four of the tools listed rather than relying on one or two? What guideline related to God's Word should we keep in mind when discerning God's will?

8. What does it mean to say that the will of God is not our happiness but our faithfulness? Has following God's will ever led you to experience hardship, difficulty, or suffering? Explain your answer.

9. Read John 17:13-21. On the night before he was crucified, what did Jesus pray for his followers? What does the word sanctify mean? (See "Leader Extra: Sanctification.") In verse 17, how did Jesus say we would be sanctified? What have you found helpful in moving your Bible study from a strictly intellectual exercise into one that shapes your attitudes and actions and affects your life?

10. Read Acts 15:1-4, 22-35. What do you think motivated the

early Christians to come together to work through their differing views? When has the fellowship and wisdom of others helped you in your faith journey—particularly in making decisions? How do you as a group help support one another in discerning God's will?

11. Are there times when we must go against the advice of our fellow believers? If so, how should we handle these times?

12. Can you name any people in the Bible who challenged—or even defied—their faith community (such as, Job, Jeremiah, Jesus)? What guidelines can help us clarify when it is better to listen to and learn from the insights of other believers? What do we lose when we try to (or are forced to) make our journey alone?

13. Read Romans 12:1-2. According to these verses, how do we live in accordance with God's will? What does it mean to offer yourself as a "living sacrifice"? In what ways are you willing to put your life—yourself—"on the altar" to live daily for God?

14. Read Romans 12:3-8. How can we renew our minds? Do you see yourself as "belonging" to all the other believers (the church)? Do you know what your special gifts and talents are? How willing have you been to offer those gifts and talents to God's work in the world?

15. Read Philippians 2:12-18. There are two kinds of "work" mentioned in these verses: God's work in us and our work (acts) to fulfill God's purpose. How would you explain or describe God's part and our part in this process?

16. How can we be confident that we are living according to God's will? What can we do to become more confident? In what ways can the spiritual disciplines of prayer, Bible reading/study, fellowship, and service help us?

17. (Note: Skip this item if you plan to do option 2 of the opening activity.) In advance, write each of the quotations from "Leader Extra: Famous Quotations on God's Will" on a separate sheet of paper or poster board, and place them all over the front wall of the room. Ask each participant to pick one quotation and share why that quotation speaks to her or him

about the will of God—or have them break into pairs for sharing if your group is large.

Group Activity

Read aloud Acts 16:1-10. Discuss: *How did God guide Paul—both directly and indirectly? Do you believe we can forge ahead with our lives and still be receptive to God's direction?*

Break into small groups of three to five persons and share in response to the following questions: *What are some ways we can be sensitive to God's nudges? What are some ways we can be instruments of God for others? How can we know when God is wanting us to move in a certain direction?*

WRAPPING UP

Notable Quotation

God's intention is that our story be about redemption and love, faith and courage. There are twists and turns in this story, and there are times we take the story in a direction God would not have chosen. There are chapters in which we do all the writing, but the best chapters are those in which we hear God's inspiration and ideas and we write the story of our lives together.

—Adam Hamilton

Closing Prayer

Lord God, life is messy and complicated. Sometimes we face tough choices and hard situations, and we wish you would step in and tell us what to do. If only you would write us a message in the sky! We often shrink from the hard work of identifying options, weighing them against your values, and making decisions. But we are so grateful that your grace frees us to be creative, to try things and take risks, and to "live out loud," trusting your love. If we go off track, you catch us and set us on our feet again. Thank you for trusting us, giving us room to fail, and teaching us to trust ourselves—because we are relying on you. Amen.

4. WHY GOD'S LOVE PREVAILS

*Main Idea: God walks with us through difficult times,
uses us to care for one another in the midst of suffering,
and forces evil and suffering to serve God
and bring about good.*

GETTING STARTED

Session Goals
This session is intended to help participants . . .

- review the ideas shared in the previous sessions about how God works in our world;
- recognize that it is normal to feel a bit less certain, safe, or secure when questioning what we know about how God works in our world;
- consider how our faith in God sustains us and gives us hope; and
- explore four truths that demonstrate God's love prevails:
    1) God walks with us.
    2) God works through us.
    3) God forces evil and suffering to serve us.
    4) God ultimately will deliver us.

Opening Prayer
Dear God, we are grateful for the opportunity we've had during this study to stretch ourselves by questioning our assumptions about the way you work in the world. Even though there is much we do not

understand, what we do know for certain is that you promise always to be with us and to work in and through us for our own good and the good of others. You even promise to redeem our suffering, bringing something beautiful from something painful. We also know that one day you will triumph over evil and suffering and deliver us. Thank you, Lord, for this hope. It is the anchor of our souls! Amen.

Biblical Foundation

We know that God works all things together for good for the ones who love God, for those who are called according to his purpose. . . . Who will separate us from Christ's love? Will we be separated by trouble, or distress, or harassment, or famine, or nakedness, or danger, or sword? . . . But in all these things we win a sweeping victory through the one who loved us. I'm convinced that nothing can separate us from God's love in Christ Jesus our Lord: not death or life, not angels or rulers, not present things or future things, not powers or height or depth, or any other thing that is created. (Romans 8:28, 35, 37-39 CEB)

Opening Activity

Ask: *Why is fear a fundamental part of the human condition?* After briefly discussing participants' answers, divide a board or chart into three columns, labeling the columns from left to right with the following headings: 1) Fears, 2) Natural Responses, 3) The Christian Response.

1. Have participants name some of the fears we face. List these in column 1.
2. Have participants identify the ways we tend to respond to these fears as human beings. List their ideas in column 2. Spend a few minutes talking about how these natural responses affect our lives.
3. Now ask: *What is the Christian response to the problem of fear?* Answers might include faith and trust in God, prayer, peace, and hope. Write the responses in column 3. Say, *In this session, we will explore how it is possible to have peace, hope, and even joy in the midst of difficulties, hardships, and suffering.*

LEARNING TOGETHER

Video Presentation
Play the DVD segment for Session 4, *Why God's Love Prevails*.
Running Time: 7:37 minutes

Key Insights
1. One of the primary affirmations of Scripture is that God is with us always. Even in times of suffering, God is with us, sustaining us and holding us in arms of love. Knowing this gives us peace in the midst of life's storms.
2. God promises to work through us to come to the aid of others in need. God is constantly working in our lives for the benefit of others and in others' lives to care for us.
3. God's primary way of working in our world is through people. Our job is to make ourselves available to God and others each day and to pay attention.
4. Suffering is inherent in life, but God uses it for God's purposes. When we place our sorrows and suffering in God's hands, we find that God redeems the suffering and uses it for our good.
5. The greatest example of God's work through suffering is the death and resurrection of Jesus Christ.
6. Ultimately hardship and suffering, evil and sin will not have the final word; that is the overwhelming message of the resurrection of Jesus Christ.
7. Though we cannot escape difficulties and pain in this life, we can know that they will not be the final word; and that gives us hope.
8. Our faith that God will ultimately prevail leads us to live boldly and without fear.

Leader Extra
Jesus' Teachings on Helping Others

Jesus both taught and demonstrated by his own example that the essence of love is to help those who are in need. Helping people was something he did on a daily basis. Whenever Jesus encountered people in need—whether they approached him or he encountered them—he always found time to stop what he was doing to help them. He taught his followers to do the same.

In the parable of the Good Samaritan (Luke 10:25-37), Jesus taught that we are to love others by meeting their needs—including those we might consider to be unworthy or even our enemies. Likewise, in the parable of the Sheep and Goats (Matthew 25:31-46), Jesus said that whoever helps those in need—whether they are in need of food and water, shelter, clothes, medical care, or even companionship—are blessed. He said that whatever we do for one of the "least of these," we do for him.

On many other occasions, Jesus instructed those who would follow him to meet the needs of others:

Give to those who ask, and don't refuse those who wish to borrow from you. (Matthew 5:42 CEB)

Sell your possessions and give to those in need. Make for yourselves wallets that don't wear out-- a treasure in heaven that never runs out. No thief comes near there, and no moth destroys. Where your treasure is, there your heart will be too. (Luke 12:33-34 CEB)

Cure the sick, raise the dead, cleanse the lepers, cast out demons. You received without payment; give without payment. (Matthew 10:8)

You lack one thing: go, sell all that you own, and give the money to the poor, and you will have treasure in heaven; then come, follow me. (Mark 10:21)

When we reach out in love to serve others, we become the hands, feet, and voice of Jesus Christ in a hurting world.

Group Discussion
Note: More questions are provided than you may have time for. Select those you would like your group to discuss.

1. Have your ideas about how God works in our world changed since beginning this study? If so, how?
2. Read Joshua 1:9, Isaiah 41:10, and Psalm 23:4. What do these verses promise? Use a Bible concordance to locate other passages of Scripture that tell us God is with us. Read the verses aloud. How or why does being aware of God's presence give us a "peace . . . which surpasses all understanding" (Philippians 4:7)? When and how have you experienced this kind of peace in your own life?
3. Read Psalm 55:22. What does this verse tell us to do? What does it promise that God will do in response? What does it mean for God to sustain you? How is this different from deliverance? How has God sustained you through a difficult time?
4. Would you agree that the primary way God works in the world and accomplishes God's will is through people? Why or why not? Why is it important for us to be available and to pay attention?
5. When have you felt that an "interruption" or "coincidence" was a God-incident—a time when God used you in the life of someone else? How did you sense God calling or nudging you to become involved?
6. How does being a part of God's work in the lives of others also bless us? How have you personally been blessed in being used by God in someone else's life?
7. What can you do to make yourself available to God each day? How can you "pay attention" to God in the midst of the busyness of life so that you are available for God-incidents?
8. Read Proverbs 31:8-9 and Isaiah 58:6-7. What are we called

to do in these verses? Which cause or call speaks to you most loudly, and why? What are some practical ways you could respond to this call?

9. Do you believe that God always redeems suffering—brings good from it? Why or why not? What Scriptures or biblical examples can you give in support of your position?

10. In what ways does all of creation seem to follow the rhythm in which new life and beauty are born out of destruction and pain? Discuss several examples.

11. Read Isaiah 61:3. What promises does God make to those who mourn and grieve in Zion? Has God ever transformed something painful from your past into something beautiful? Share as you are willing.

12. Why are the death and resurrection of Jesus Christ the greatest example of God's work through suffering?

13. How can we be sure that good ultimately will triumph over evil? How does this belief give us hope?

14. Read 1 Peter 3:15. How would you explain the hope that you have?

Group Activity

Divide into two or more small groups, depending on your class size. Assign each group one or more of the following Scriptures:

Lamentations 3:21-23
Jeremiah 29:11
Isaiah 51:11
1 Corinthians 15:54-58
2 Corinthians 4:16–5:1
Revelation 21:1-5

Have the groups read the Scripture(s) and discuss the following: *How does this Scripture give us hope? How does it inspire us to live boldly and without fear? In what ways do you sense God calling you to live more boldly? What changes will this require?*

Come back together and have a member of each group share a brief summary of their Scripture(s) and thoughts.

WRAPPING UP

Notable Quotation

Every day I pray for my children. . . . When I pray for them I find peace. My peace doesn't come from believing that since I prayed for them nothing bad will ever happen to them. I hope for this, but I have officiated at the funerals of enough young people to know that it doesn't always work that way. My peace comes from knowing that God is with them, and that even if something terrible happens, God will be by their side, holding them and sustaining them and, should the worst thing happen, God will still hold them in arms of love.   —Adam Hamilton

Closing Prayer

Lord God, as we journey through life, each of us will experience difficulty, pain, and suffering. These realities are a part of life. No one is exempt. Essentially we have two choices in the face of suffering: to despair of life or to find hope and peace through faith in You. In order to choose faith, we have to ask ourselves this question: "Do I really believe the story about the Resurrection?" We must decide if we believe that, because of Jesus' resurrection, evil and suffering do not have the last word—that ultimately good will triumph and God's plans will prevail. Help us, God, not only to believe this but to count on it! Amen.

ENDNOTES

1. *When Christians Get It Wrong*, Adam Hamilton (Abingdon Press, 2010), see pages 70-71.

2. *When Christians Get It Wrong, Leader Guide* (Abingdon Press, 2010), p. 46. Used by permission.

3. *When Christians Get It Wrong*, pp. 67-72. Used by permission.

4. *When Christians Get It Wrong, Leader Guide*, pp. 46-48. Used by permission.

ENOUGH

Money has great power in our lives. Used wisely, it is one key to accomplishing our goals, providing for our needs, and fulfilling our life purpose. However, ignoring the wisdom of the past when it comes to managing and spending our money can lead to greater stress and anxiety. *Enough* is an invitation to rediscover the Bible's wisdom when it comes to prudent financial practices. In its pages are found the keys to experiencing contentment, overcoming fear, and discovering joy through simplicity and generosity.

Read *Enough* on your own or, for a more in-depth study, enjoy it with a small group.

ISBN 978-1-5018-5788-1

"We Americans love our stuff. We're living in a fast-paced, me-first, instant-gratification world, and it's finally catching up to us. Debt is out of control, homes are in foreclosure ... even banks are going out of business. What the world needs today is the message of contentment and simplicity, and that's exactly what Pastor Adam Hamilton delivers in *Enough*."
—**Dave Ramsey**, *New York Times* Best-Selling Author and Nationally Syndicated Radio Talk Show Host

Available wherever fine books are sold.
For more information about Adam Hamilton, visit www.AdamHamilton.org

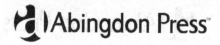

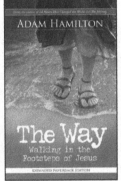

CPSIA information can be obtained
at www.ICGtesting.com
Printed in the USA
LVHW041455130220
646864LV00008B/1384